Africa's Most Dangerous!

The Big 5

TJ Rob

THE BIG 5 - Africa's Most Dangerous

By TJ Rob

Copyright Text TJ Rob, 2016
All rights reserved. No part of the book may be reproduced in any form without permission in writing from the author. Reviewers may quote brief passages in review.
ISBN 978-1-988695-44-0

Disclaimer
No part of this book may be reproduced in any form or by any means, mechanical or electronic, including photocopying or recording, or by an information storage and retrieval system, or transmitted by email without permission in writing from the publisher. This book is for entertainment purposes only. The views expressed are those of author alone.

Published by:
TJ Rob
Suite 609
440-10816 Macleod Trail SE
Calgary, AB T2J 5N8   www.TJRob.com

Photo Credits: Images used under license from Flickr.com, Public Domain, Wikimedia Commons: Front Cover, Daughter#3 CC BY-SA 2.0 / Wikimedia Commons; Front Cover, David Berkowitz / Flickr.com; Front Cover, Mike / Flickr.com; Front Cover, Franco Pecchio / Flickr.com; Front Cover, Megan Coughlin / Flickr.com; pg. 1, Daughter#3 CC BY-SA 2.0 / Wikimedia Commons; pg. 1, David Berkowitz / Flickr.com; pg. 1, Mike / Flickr.com; pg. 1, Franco Pecchio / Flickr.com; pg. 1, Megan Coughlin / Flickr.com; pg. 6, William Warby / Flickr.com; pg. 6, Danh CC BY-SA 3.0 / via Wikimedia Commons; pg. 6, Mike / Flickr.com; pg. 6, Wj32 CC-BY-SA-3.0 / via Wikimedia Commons; pg. 6, Megan Coughlin / Flickr.com; pg. 7, Akash_Kurdekar / Flickr.com; pg. 8, Photocreo Bednarek - Fotolia.com; pg. 9, Laura Galbraith - Fotolia.com; pg. 10, gi0572 - Fotolia.com; pg. 11, gudkovandrey - Fotolia.com; pg. 12, Mark Bridger/bridgephotography - Fotolia.com; pg. 13, dennisjacobsen - Fotolia.com; pg. 14, Stu Porter Photography - Fotolia.com; pg. 15, VOLODYMYR BURDYAK - Fotolia.com; pg. 16, Brian Fitzharris / Flickr.com; pg. 17, Tony Campbell - Fotolia.com; pg. 18, GrantRyan - Fotolia.com; pg. 19, Dmitry Balakirev - Fotolia.com; pg. 20, Donovan van Staden - Fotolia.com; pg. 21, bradleyvdw - Fotolia.com; pg. 22, amanderson2 / Flickr.com; pg. 23, Vidu Gunaratna AČK - Fotolia.com; pg. 24, Bernard DUPONT CC BY-SA 2.0 / Wikimedia Commons ; pg. 25, Duncan Noakes - Fotolia.com; pg. 26, Mike / Flickr.com; pg. 27, Volodymyr Burdiak - Fotolia.com; pg. 28, Nico Smit - Fotolia.com; pg. 29, Four Oaks - Fotolia.com; pg. 30, scooperdigital - Fotolia.com; pg. 31, ryan harvey CC BY-SA 2.0 / Wikimedia Commons; pg. 32, Franco Pecchio / Flickr.com; pg. 33, sidliks - Fotolia.com; pg. 34, catfish07 - Fotolia.com; pg. 35, bondsza - Fotolia.com; pg. 36, Max Handelsman / Flickr.com; pg. 37, Charlesjsharp CC BY-SA 3.0 / Wikimedia Commons; pg. 38, okyela - Fotolia.com; pg. 39, valerieBaron / Pixabay.com

TABLE OF CONTENTS   Page

Visit www.TJRob.com for more exciting books   4

What are Africa's Big 5 Animals?   6

Where does the name Big 5 come from?   7

Lion   8

Do You know these Lion Facts?   13

Leopard   14

Do you know these Leopard Facts?   19

Cape Buffalo   20

Do you know these Cape Buffalo Facts?   26

Rhino   27

Do you know these Rhino Facts?   32

Elephants   33

Do you know these Elephant Facts?   39

Thanks for Reading — More exciting books from TJ Rob   40

Visit www.TJRob.com for other exciting books by TJ Rob:

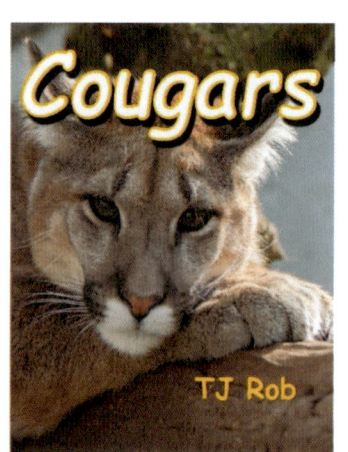
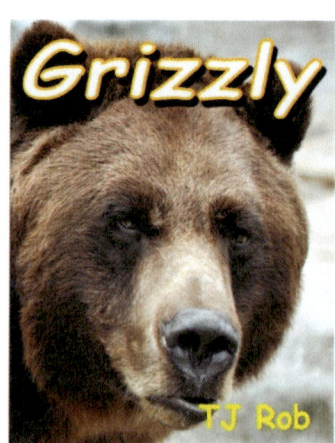
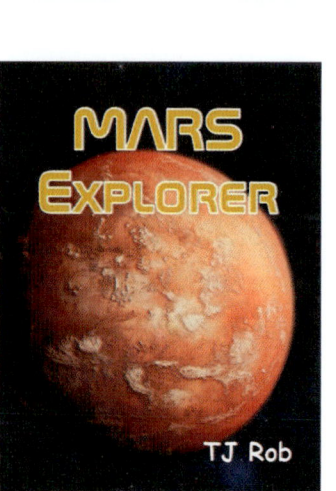

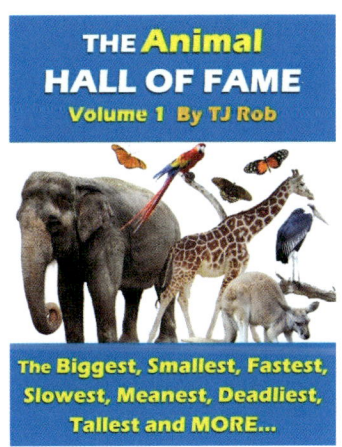

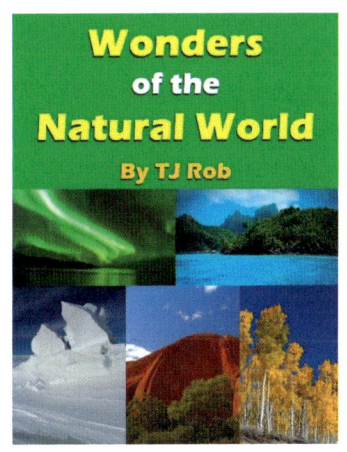
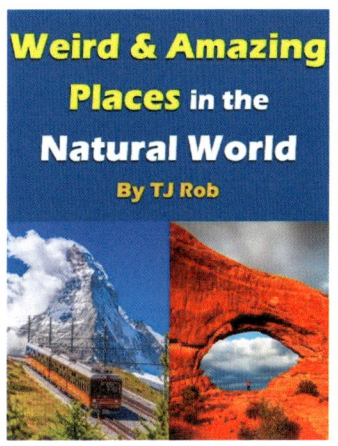
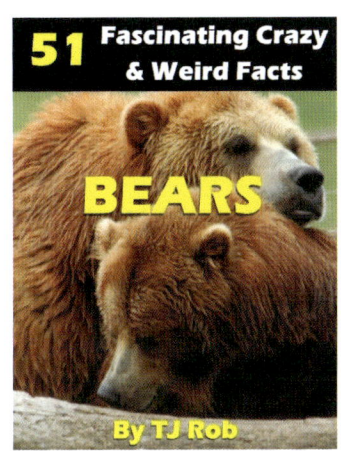
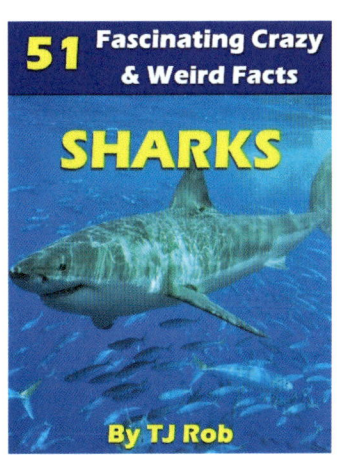
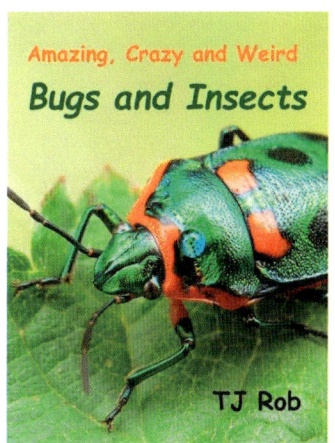

What are Africa's BIG 5 Animals?

Lion

Leopard

Elephant

Cape Buffalo

Rhino

Where does the name BIG 5 come from?

About 100 years ago, the "Big 5" were thought of as the 5 most dangerous animals that big game hunters used to hunt on foot.

The name stuck, but the shooting we do today is done using cameras instead of guns.

The Big 5 are also some of the most amazing creatures that have amazing abilities and can do amazing things.

Let's explore some little known facts about the "Big 5".

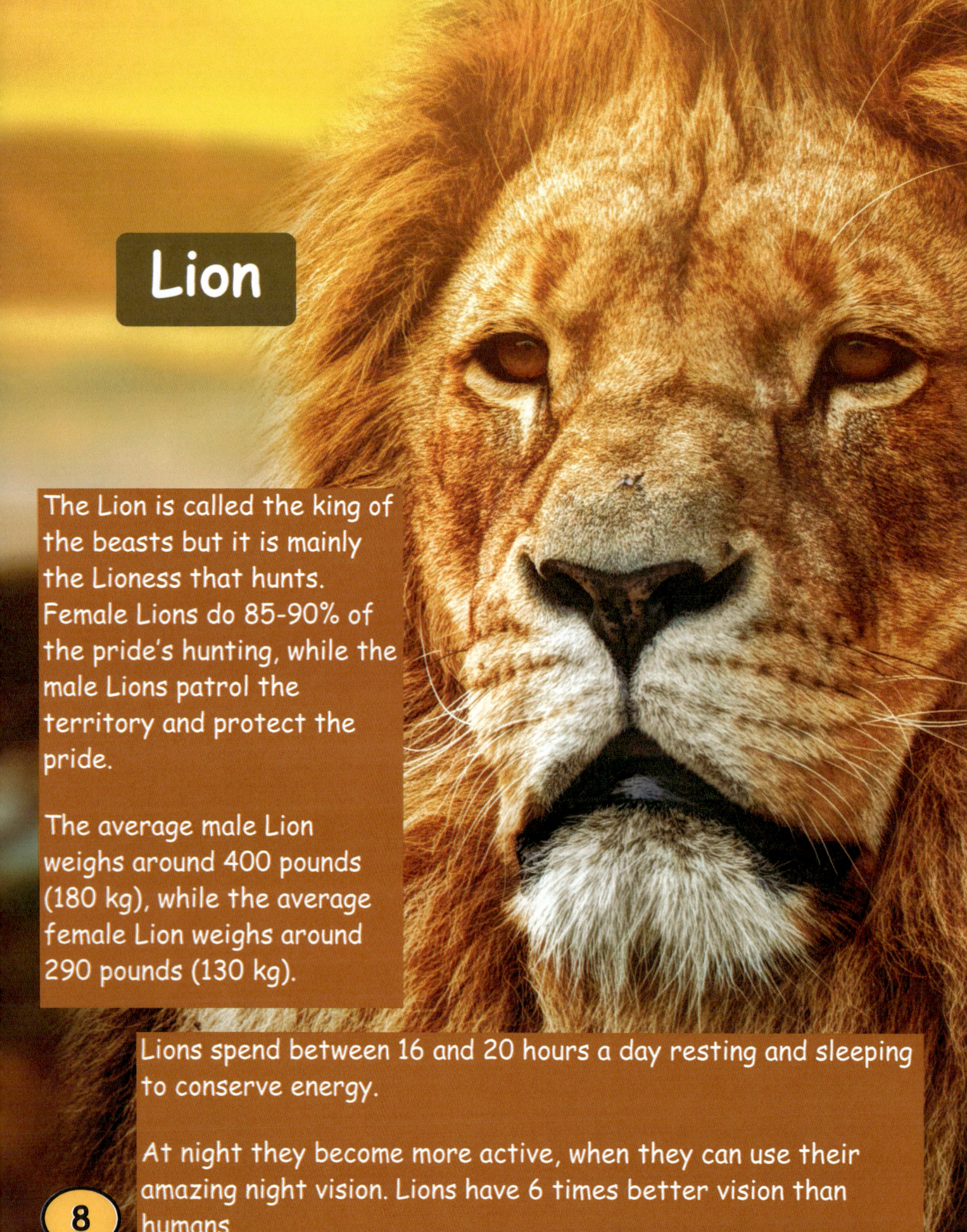

Lion

The Lion is called the king of the beasts but it is mainly the Lioness that hunts. Female Lions do 85-90% of the pride's hunting, while the male Lions patrol the territory and protect the pride.

The average male Lion weighs around 400 pounds (180 kg), while the average female Lion weighs around 290 pounds (130 kg).

Lions spend between 16 and 20 hours a day resting and sleeping to conserve energy.

At night they become more active, when they can use their amazing night vision. Lions have 6 times better vision than humans.

Lions can reach speeds of up to 50 miles per hour (81 kilometers per hour) but only in short bursts because they lack stamina.

Unlike Cheetahs, Lions are built for power but not for speed.

Lions give up after 300 feet (100 meters) of chasing a prey.

Lions can also leap as far as 36 feet (11 meters) when pouncing on their prey.

They have such powerful jaws that when they have their prey in their jaws they seldom let go, until they have strangled their prey.

Lions hunt large animals such as zebra and wildebeest.

The average life expectancy for Lions is 12 years for males and 15 years for females.

A lion's roar can be heard up to 5 miles (7 km) away. Both males and females are able to roar.

Once Lions roamed across most of Africa and even parts of Europe and Asia.

In the 1940s there were 450,000 Lions in the wild.

Nowadays the world's remaining Lion population only lives in the Southern parts of Africa.

Today, there are as few as 32,000 wild Lions on Earth.

No other big cats have a mane. It makes the male Lion appear larger and more scary.

It also signals maturity and health status. Lionesses tend to prefer thicker and darker manes.

Lions live in family groups, or prides, of between 15 and 25 animals. A pride is normally made up of Lionesses and cubs, with one or two male Lions.

Lionesses are caring mothers. They will even take care of a neglected cub, allowing him/her to suckle and giving them a chance to survive. Two or more Lionesses in a group tend to give birth around the same time and the cubs are raised together.

At birth Lion cubs only weigh about 3 pounds(1.37 kg).

Vulnerable to predators like Hyenas, Leopards, and Black-backed Jackals, cubs have a 30-40% chance of survival.

By the age of 2, Lions are pretty good hunters. They become fully grown between 5 and 6 years old.

Female cubs stay with the group as they age.

Young males are forced out of the pride when grown. They form bachelor groups and follow migrating herds until they are strong enough to challenge male lions of other prides.

Do you know these Lion Facts?

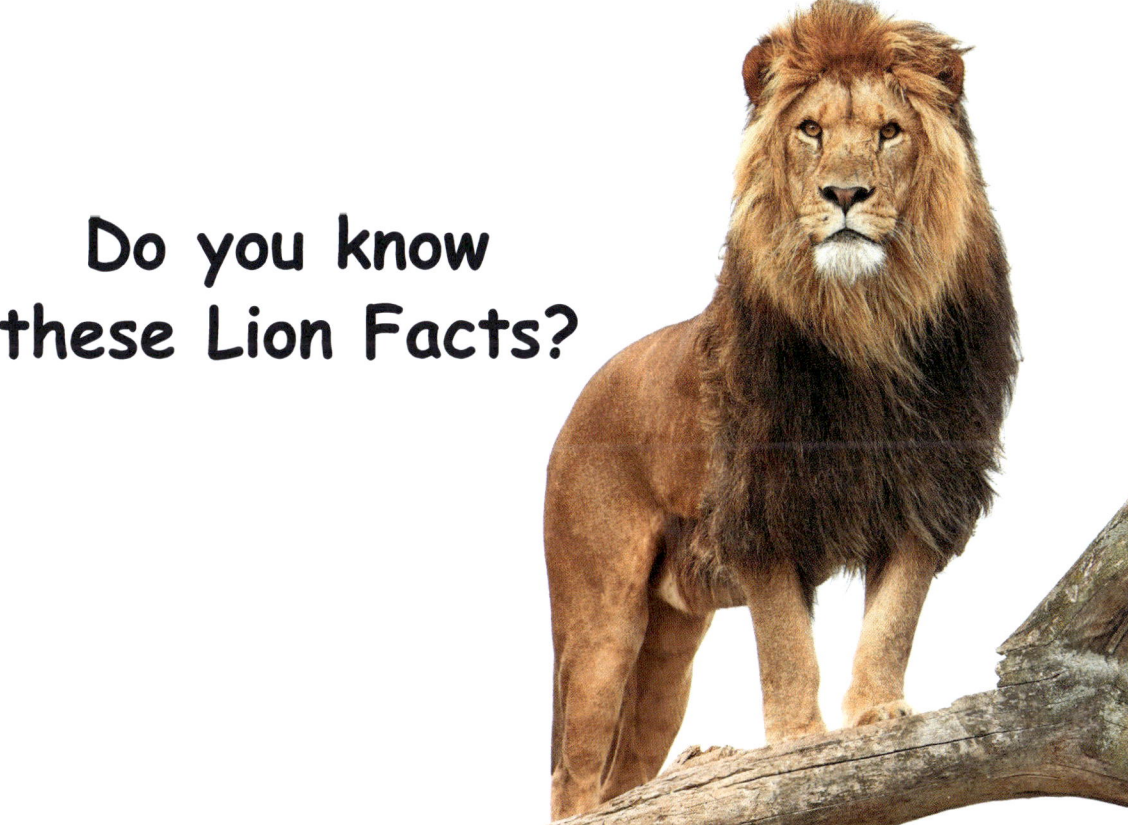

1) There are more statues of Lions in the world than there are real wild Lions.

2) Until they reach 2 years old, Lions can't roar.

3) Although they do not naturally see people as prey, Lions have been known to sneak into villages to find food. Lions attack up to 700 people every year, causing 100 deaths in Tanzania alone.

4) In 1898, two Lions in Kenya became famous for killing and eating over 130 rail-road workers over a 9 month period.

5) Lions are the national animal of several countries, including Albania, Belgium, Bulgaria, England, Ethiopia, Luxembourg, the Netherlands, and Singapore.

Leopard

African Leopards have a wide range in size and weight.

Males weigh from 66 to 200 pounds (30 to 90 kg). Females weigh from 51 to 123 pounds (23 to 60 kg).

Leopards are amazing tree climbers and good runners.

They are able to carry dead prey weighing twice or even three times their own body weight 20 feet (6 meters) up a tree.

They often leave their dead prey up a tree for days at a time, returning to eat when they are hungry.

Leopards are amazing stalkers. They stalk to within 15 feet (5 metres) of their prey and then leap onto them in a surprise attack.

Leopards eat small hoofed animals such as Gazelle, Impala, Deer and Wildebeest. They may also hunt Monkeys, Rodents and Birds.

Leopards sleep in hiding during most of the day and come out to hunt at night using their fantastic night vision.

A Leopard's night vision is up to 7 times better than a human's, and its hearing is up to 5 times better.

Unlike Lions that live in prides, Leopards mainly live alone and have large territories. Their territories can sometimes be a as large as 60 square miles (100 square km).

Leopard mothers have 2 or 3 cubs at a time.

The cubs are born with their eyes shut to protect against sunlight and prevent the cubs from wandering. Within two weeks their eyes are open.

Leopard cubs are kept hidden for the first 8 weeks of their lives. They are hidden in dens and moved regularly from one den to another by the mother Leopard. Mother Leopards do this to protect their cubs, possibly to avoid the build-up of scent that might attract predators or to prevent the build-up of ticks and fleas.

Cubs stay with their mothers until they are about 2 years old. This is when they are old enough to hunt and take care of themselves.

Most Leopards are light colored and have dark spots on their fur. These spots are called 'rosettes' because their shape is similar to that of a rose.

No two Leopards have the same markings or color. They are as unique as human fingerprints.

A Leopard's tail can reach almost 3 feet (1 meter) in length. It has a white tip at the end of its tail. When a mother Leopard takes her cubs through undergrowth or long grass, she holds her tail upright. Cubs then follow their mother by looking out for the white tip of the tail, even at nighttime.

A Leopard also has long whiskers that it uses as antennae to judge spaces between bushes and trees. Very useful for an animal that hunts at night.

Although Leopards in Asia are critically endangered, the African Leopard is not and it is estimated that there are close to 500,000 wild Leopards in existence.

That is nearly ten times the number of all wild Lions, Tigers and Cheetahs combined.

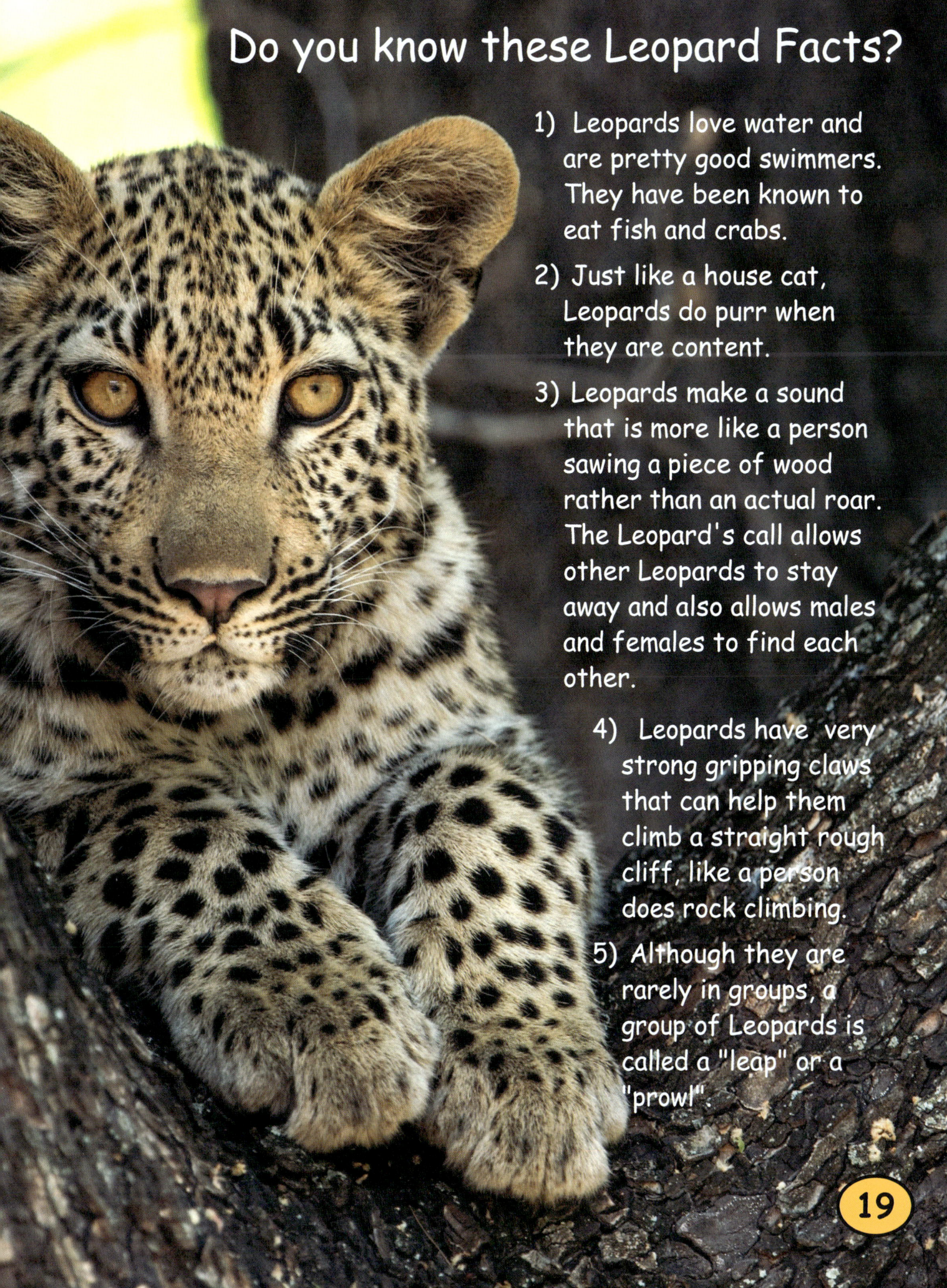

Do you know these Leopard Facts?

1) Leopards love water and are pretty good swimmers. They have been known to eat fish and crabs.

2) Just like a house cat, Leopards do purr when they are content.

3) Leopards make a sound that is more like a person sawing a piece of wood rather than an actual roar. The Leopard's call allows other Leopards to stay away and also allows males and females to find each other.

4) Leopards have very strong gripping claws that can help them climb a straight rough cliff, like a person does rock climbing.

5) Although they are rarely in groups, a group of Leopards is called a "leap" or a "prowl."

Cape Buffalo

Regarded as the most dangerous of the Big 5. Buffalo are said to have killed more hunters in Africa than any other wild animal.

Buffalos have good memories and are known to ambush hunters that have harmed them in the past.

 An adult Buffalo can easily weigh about 1,500 pounds (700kg).

Buffalo herds constantly move around looking for new grazing.

Cape Buffalo need to drink water daily, often in the early morning and late afternoon. It is at these times that you can find hundreds of Buffalo at water holes.

They prefer to eat tall, coarse grass as well as bushes and form large herds all moving together.

They do most of their grazing at night, in the early morning and in the evening so that they can escape the heat of the day by standing or lying in shade.

To obtain minerals and trace elements they lick termite mounds and the mud stuck to their companions.

The Buffalo's primary predator is the Lion. Lions are wary of preying on Buffalo unless they are hunting in groups. This might seem surprising when you see Buffalo in their natural habitat. They seem quite calm and peaceful. When danger appears and they feel threatened,

Buffalo are animals that not even a Lion should mess with!

Buffalo will try to rescue another member who has been caught. Buffalo have been known to kill a Lion after it has killed a member of the herd.

African Buffalos live in large herds, sometimes consisting of thousands of animals.

Herds usually consist of females, their offspring and one or more males. Males that are not part of the herd can form bachelor herds, or live a solitary life.

Solitary animals are an easy target for Lions, which are their natural enemies.

Life in a herd ensures certain advantages. Animals are well informed about the best feeding areas and sources of water. Besides that, they are protected against the predators.

When faced with predators, the animals of the herd form a circle around the young, old or weak animals, exposing their large and sharp horns toward the predators. This barrier is very effective and prevents predators from reaching the animals that are not strong enough to fight.

Cape Buffalos have rather bad sight and hearing, making them unpredictable and dangerous animals to approach. On the other hand, their sense of smell is excellent. This super sense of smell helps them find food and alert them to danger.

The male bulls fight each other for position in the herd. They clash and crash into each other's horns. The impact of two bulls butting heads is like a car hitting a wall at 30 miles an hour (50 km/h).

The mating season of Cape Buffalo takes place between March and May. Pregnancy lasts 11 and a half months and ends with one baby (calf). The bond between mother and calf is very strong. The calf is completely dependent on its mother during its first years of life.

Male calves leave their mothers when they reach 2 years old. Female calves stay in the herd until they produce their own offspring at about 5 years old.

Do you know these Cape Buffalo Facts?

1) Unlike Asian Water Buffalo, African Buffalo have never been tamed.

2) A Buffalo is 4 times stronger than an Ox.

3) Buffalo are capable swimmers and often cross deep water in search of better grazing.

4) The average lifespan of the Cape Buffalo in the wild is 20 years.

Rhino

Rhinos are the 2nd largest land mammal on Earth.

Rhinos can weigh up to 7700 pounds (3500 kg). They stand up to 6 feet (1.8 meters) tall at the shoulders.

They can live up to 40 to 45 years of age in the wild.

Two species of Rhino live in Africa—the White Rhino and the Black Rhino. The other three types – Indian, Sumatran and Java Rhino are all found in Asia.

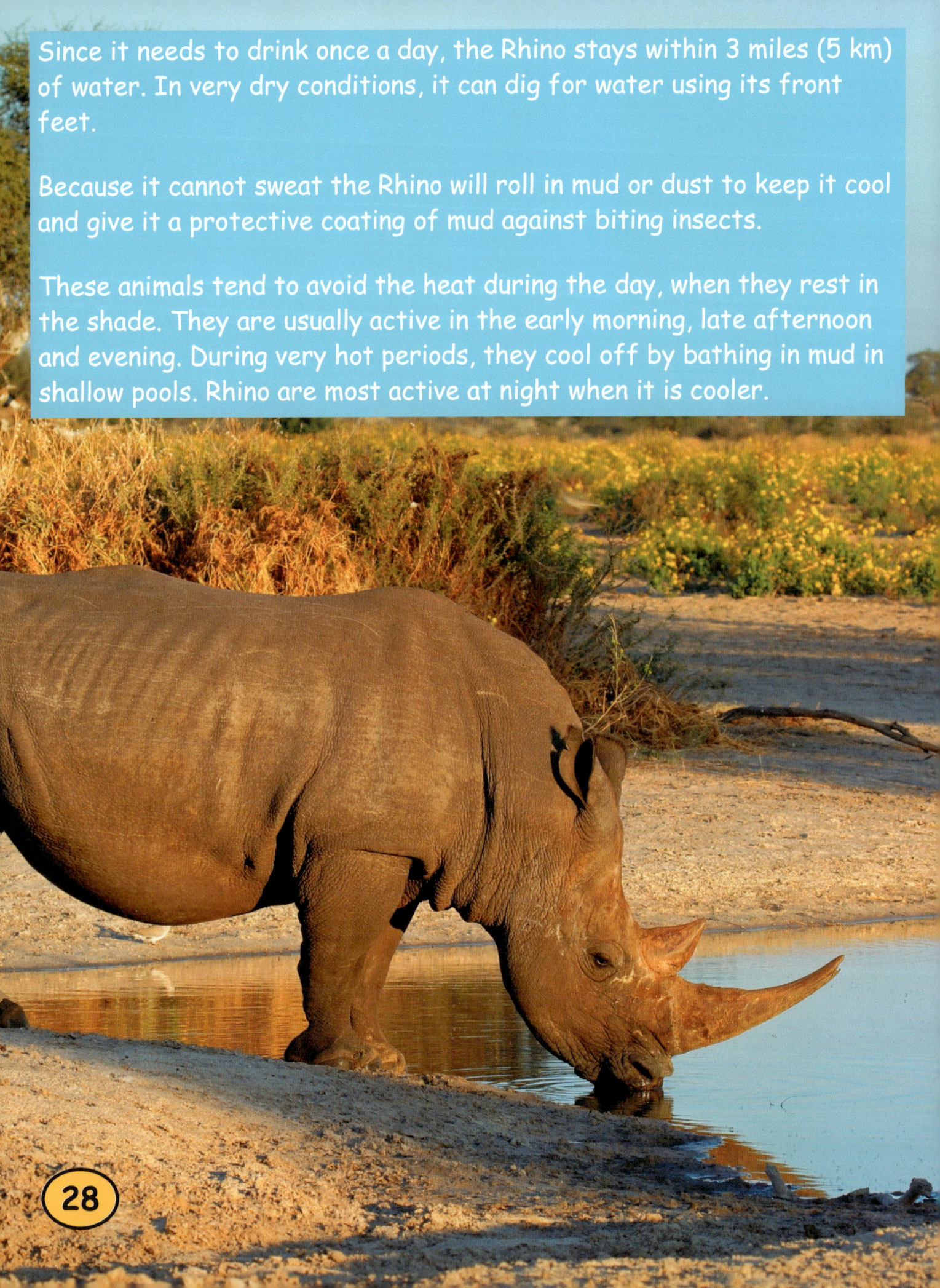

Since it needs to drink once a day, the Rhino stays within 3 miles (5 km) of water. In very dry conditions, it can dig for water using its front feet.

Because it cannot sweat the Rhino will roll in mud or dust to keep it cool and give it a protective coating of mud against biting insects.

These animals tend to avoid the heat during the day, when they rest in the shade. They are usually active in the early morning, late afternoon and evening. During very hot periods, they cool off by bathing in mud in shallow pools. Rhino are most active at night when it is cooler.

Rhino pregnancy is long at between 15 to 16 months and produces 1 calf. Young Rhinos can walk 10 minutes after they are born.

However, the mother will keep the calf hidden for a couple of weeks in fear that it may get trampled upon. Rhino calves weigh about 100 pounds (45 kg) at birth.

Rhinos stop growing when about 7 years old.

A Rhino calf stays with its mother until it is about 2 to 4 years old, when she has her next calf. In the wild she will have just one calf every 2 to 5 years.

The mother always leads the calf and will defend it against actual and potential danger. Cows with calves are especially dangerous and will charge when feeling threatened. Although they nurse for 1 year, calves are able to begin eating vegetation a few weeks after birth. The calf stays around until its mother pushes it away when its sibling is born.

Rhinos have really poor eyesight. They sometimes attack trees and rocks that are only a few feet (meters) away mistaking them for other animals.

But a great sense of smell and great hearing make up for their bad eyesight. They can probably smell a human from at least 600 feet (200 meters) away.

Full grown Rhinos have few predators, other than man. Calves are in more danger. A Lion may try to take a Rhino calf.

For short distances Rhinos can run as fast a horse, reaching speeds of 40 miles per hour (60 km per hour).

They are also able to turn sharply in a small space.

Do you know these Rhino Facts?

1) A group of Rhinos is called a crash.

2) Rhino horns are made of keratin - the same material that nails, claws and hooves are made of. The longest measured Rhino horn was 4 feet and 9 inches (1.45 meters) long.

3) White Rhinos are not white in color. The early Dutch settlers used the word for wide "Wyd". The name became misinterpreted for the English word "white". The name stuck.

4) All rhinos have 3 toes on each foot.

5) Rhinos have been around for over 50 million years. They haven't changed much since prehistoric times.

Elephant

Elephants are the biggest of all land animals on earth – often weighing 15,450 pounds (7000 kg).

Many Elephants live for 70 years.

The oldest known Elephant lived until he was 83 years old.

African Elephants are bigger and heavier than their Asian Elephant cousins.

Elephants are highly social and live in family groups of about 25 animals of all ages. The leader of the herd is normally an older female Elephant called the matriarch. The herd follow her everywhere.

Elephants have the longest pregnancy of all mammals, almost 22 months. Newborn calves weigh around 200 pounds (90 kg) and are about 3 feet tall.

The males leave the herd when they reach about 12 years old and join other young males in a male herd of their own.

Elephants have amazing memories. The matriarch and fellow senior females remember information such as the location of waterholes which allows Elephants to survive in the long dry periods.

Elephants communicate with each other through touch, sound and scent. They use a wide range of sounds to talk to each other, and even communicate at low frequencies which humans can't hear.

Elephants are able to recognize themselves using mirrors. Only cretaceans, magpies, humans and other primates have so far been found to recognize themselves in mirrors.

Elephants are highly sensitive creatures. They will help a fallen or injured Elephant. There is even evidence that Elephants mourn the death of their loved ones.

An elephant's trunk is incredibly strong and powerful. It can lift up huge logs and trees that weigh up to 750 pounds (340 kg) with its trunk.

The trunk is also nimble and sensitive. It is capable of lifting elephant calves, but can also pluck a flower.

The trunk is filled with thousands of tiny muscles that allows it to move in almost any direction.

Elephants use their trunks to breathe and make noises like trumpeting.

They also use their trunks to feel and understand the size and shape of things.

Most importantly, they use their trunks to suck up water to put in their mouths to drink.

The large ears of African Elephants help to keep the animals cool in the often brutal African heat.

African Elephants spend much of their time roaming over wide areas in search of enough food. They only spend about 4 hours a day sleeping.

Elephants eat up to 300 pounds (136 kg) of fruit, bark, roots and grasses every day.

Their long ivory tusks are used for defending themselves from other animals, for stripping bark from trees and as a digging implement to pull up roots to eat.

Elephants are dangerous animals. Their huge size makes them capable of crushing and killing any other land animal, including Lions, and humans are also at risk.

Elephants are responsible for over 400 deaths every year in different parts of the world.

Because they are so huge, don't think of Elephants as slow. They can move at 25 miles per hour (40 km/h) for short bursts – much faster than a human can run.

They are great walkers and can easily cover 50 miles (80 km) in a single day.

Do You know these Elephant Facts?

1) African Elephants are very difficult to tame and to train. Asian Elephants are much easier.

2) Baby Elephants are born blind and some individuals suck their trunks for comfort, similar to the way young humans suck their thumbs.

3) Like us humans who are left or right handed, Elephants prefer one tusk over another.

4) Elephants have been on Earth for the last 5 to 6 million years — longer than humans.

5) The Elephant brain is the largest of all land mammals, with a mass of over 11 pounds (5 kg). It is similar in structure to the human brain.

6) Elephants do not like to eat peanuts and they are not scared of mice!

THANKS FOR READING!
Please tell others what you liked about it.

Visit www.TJRob.com to learn about other exciting books by TJ Rob

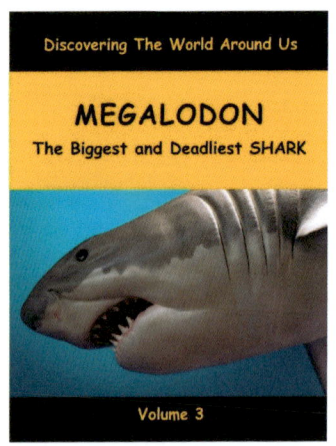
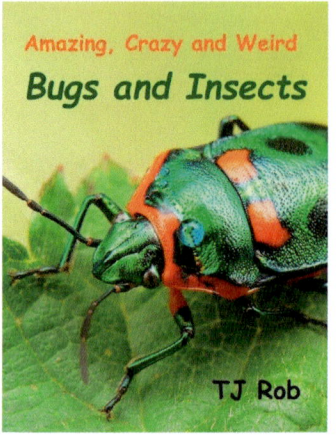
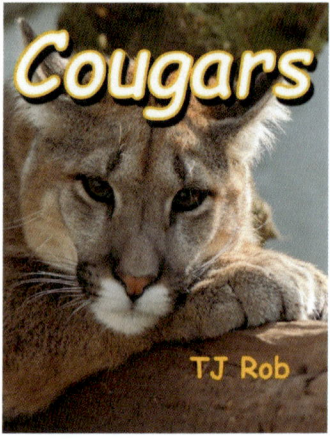

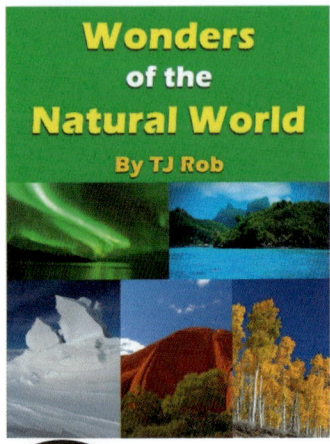
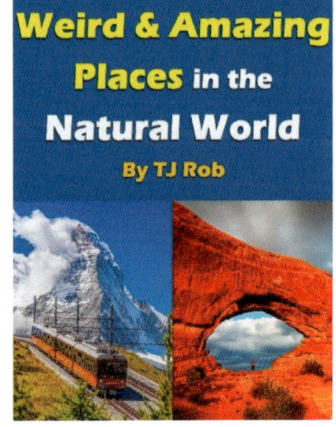

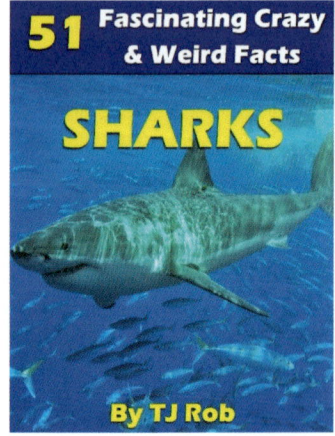

Printed in Great Britain
by Amazon